Redshift

3

© 2019 Respective Writers

All rights reserved for the author.
Please contact the author for permissions.

Arroyo Seco Press

Redshift Anthology #3

www.arroyosecopress.org

cover and interior art by Ann Brantingham

logo by Morgan G. Robles
morganrobles.carbonmade.com

ISBN-13: 978-1-7326911-2-4
ISBN-10: 1-7326911-2-6

for Michelle

Redshift

scan the heavens
focus on the darkness
life explodes

punk show

wear anything black
downing beers in parking lot
don't remember rest

Orange cat prowls nightly:
rooster, hen, scratch up breakfast—
three chicks left to feed.

we enter
flow this stream
then exit

Cinnamon and orange
tea burns my tongue leaving numb
taste buds on the tip

in the same way that your kiss
left me burning numb inside

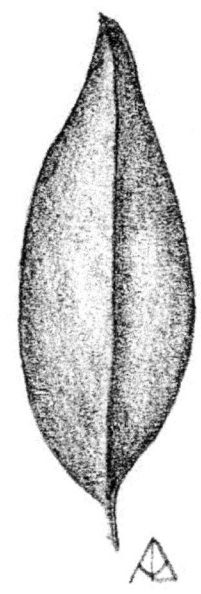

after the wind storm
gathering leaves off the pond
by swimming

in the naked
moonlight

time travel so weird
watched myself being born
cute little guy

mom radiant with joy
dad fainted dead away

We turn the front porch
Lights off at night and hope to
Keep the moths alive

Salt water on planks
warping the tangled wood grooves
like fine lines on palms

mononymiysly
yours, Death. his final letters
wilt in autumn's glow.

infinite
or just beyond
our grasp

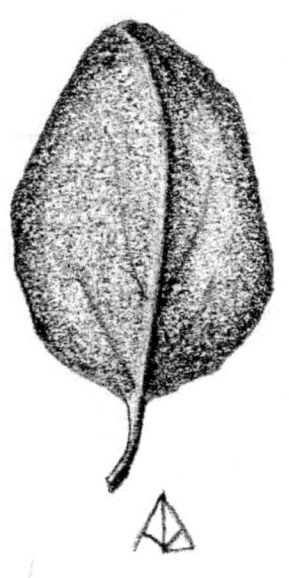

its sclera sizzles
one yellow pupil hardens
—flip it out of sight

you were never born
take comfort in the darkness
know the slow descent

Patience—an upside-down
praying mantis
on the citronella

my tent in the sand
three mattress pads
two teddy bears

Once I was found sweet,
a plum in season—women
in refrigerators

Britney Spears

Traditionally,
haiku is not supposed to
have a title, oops…

the stone makes ripples on the water
the water smooths the stone
if there is time

Bombs fall on this land.
Tanks roam through this land. No, here there are no children.

final descent
to the new planet
maroon sky

I want maps drawn out
Spider veins on leaves in light
sketched with fingernails

on the pale skin of my back
leaving pink roads leading home

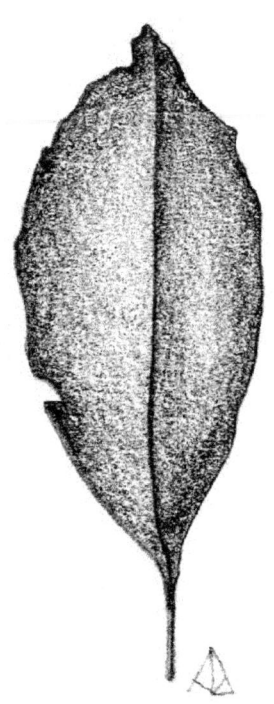

White sun warms
my eyelids and I
daydream of water.

Loons slip, dip surface
wait   wait   wait   hear the splash there
mournful cry   alone

Pierce this heart, rend flesh
turn these bones into meal, feed
heaven-traveler remains

to those hungry for anything:
it will sustain them forever

Bodysurfing

A blue sun at dawn,
The sky full of white seabirds
Searching for breakfast.

caw
        blah
            caw
                blah
even the crow
            has allergies
this spring

Do I belong here?
This mask is heavy with an
Imposter beneath.

Mt. Baldy

Rocks unknowingly
reap the joy of cold kisses
from the melting snow—

The Kiss, unfelt and unseen,
touches little lips of trust.

Me and the mulch
shelter out of the sun—
we've grown enough

The Universal Lyric

Grouse calls,
Canadians
tell me, sound like distant

mooses—proof that love
is the same all over.

Hiding Place

Relinquishing thought
to unknown darkness unfelt
seeds sprout in secret

In the morning light
Scarlet birds sit unbothered
By the old blind man.

Sing siren song   there
   upon the full lips of moon
  wavering light touches

  the dust surface and   water
 seeps from flesh   in deep longing

Motherhood is war.
We birth life through death, feed one
generation on

the thoughts of the old. Mercy
has no place in seeding life.

our mortal coil
shedding little by little
with every sunset

Black spider climbs
smooth, white walls,
inches above water.

Toothless now
like always he whistles ideas
forgets to eat

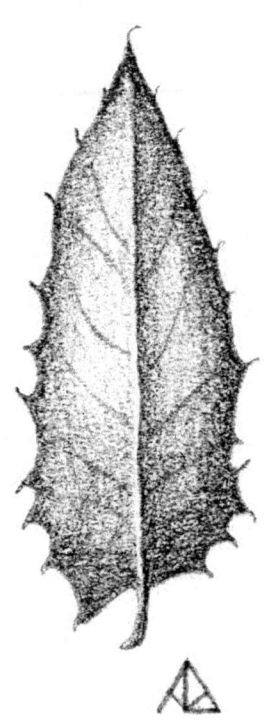

Ex-Humans

raise the boneyards, lord
let the dead all speak to me
no fear will stop me

morbid hidden in a crypt
hollowed out and alone.

In Spring,
the grouse hum love
to mates. Later, they hum

for hatchlings. Their feet track on snow
that melts.

intergalactic
planetary fun and games
excite us always

baby blanket
held together
with memories

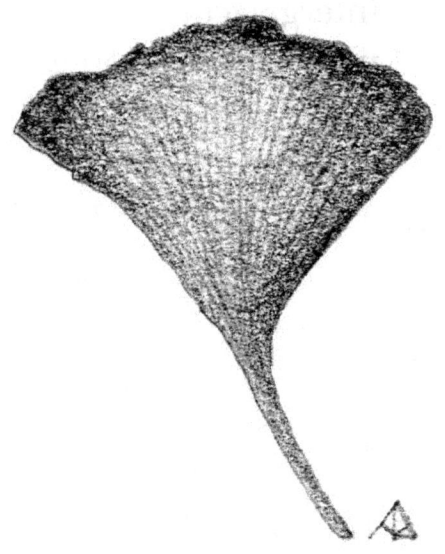

she puts on the tea
while waiting for the boil
kisses his nipples

Light rain taps tin roof—
seeds swell and sprout in the earth:
husband lies sleeping.

Bob Dylan sings of
A pretty girl in late fall,
Moving through high grass.

On the beach bird kites soar,
vendors offer passionfruit popsicles
and straw sunhats,

my mother lounges,
sucks on her cigarette.

Stillness of water
Reflects old woman image.
Lines of past turmoil.

Ex-Mom

she lost her battle
to a life support system
we had both turned off

and i counted her heart rate
the energy in her all gone

Ex-Boy

I would always hide
away from the world in dreams
behind closed curtains

television scrambling me
into a box of wild cards.

fifty-five bass on your stringer blue skies

broken branch
after her death
persimmons

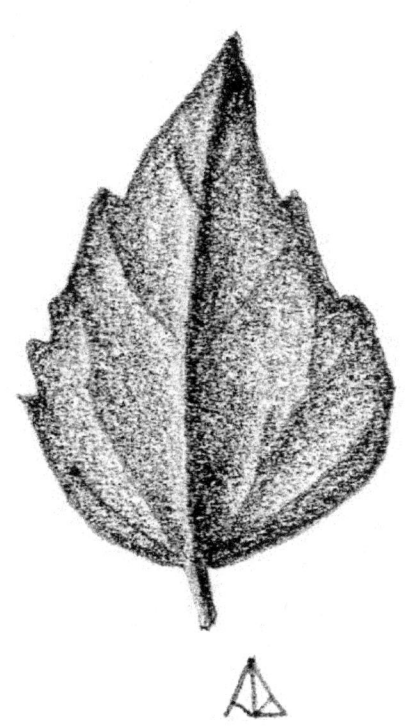

far lunar surface
Darth Vader moon bugs
their rainbow molting phase

Striped cat in sunlight
bounced beams with agility,
light limbs in joy, play,

while I practice spelling lists -
my time with mother, rare bliss.

this damn cubicle
makes me want to grab a beer
reaching for it now

Swarms of tadpoles swim
In dark, cold open water.
Spring will be here soon.

a book
halfway through
a seaweed

Museum

A nude woman looks
Back at me from the canvas,
Bright stars above her.

Outside it is late autumn,
But in here it's early spring.

sun exits
passes the moon
kissing

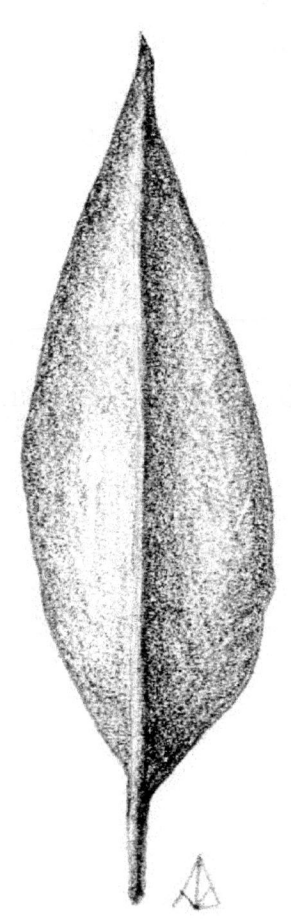

among the broken
shells, half-in-sand—another
abandoned syringe

last flames of sunset
 extinguished
  in Pacific blue

Mexico

no seatbelts in cars
riding in backs of pickups
I see no crashes

Welsh pony licks
my hand, for the salt, I think
but it feels like love

Her morning puja:
ribbon of smoke from joss sticks
carries prayers skyward.

earthquake summer
no longer feeling
the jolt

petal flurry -
my oolong tea
turns cherry

Bri-ku

I am a hybrid;
my first name mixed with art form
born onto canvas

We were both selfish,
But at least I am the one
Who admits it.

Cancelled wedding
The bride's message
Comes from

an unmonitored
mailbox.

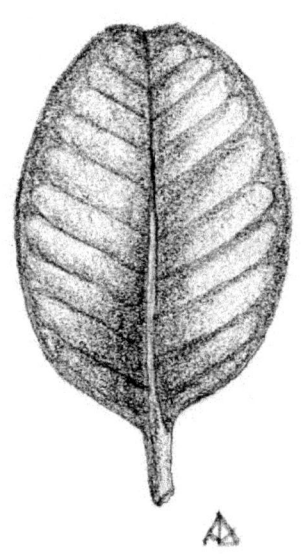

a mercurial cat
seductively feral
sub rosa in light

The tramp boils his boot
taste of leather, taste of dust
the flavor of poverty

for Charlie Chaplin

haiku are the worst
there is so much restriction
but here I am, done.

In contemplation
Of baby hummingbird souls
Nectar, tears combine

each summer we dance
as moths to forbidden flame—
the shape of risk

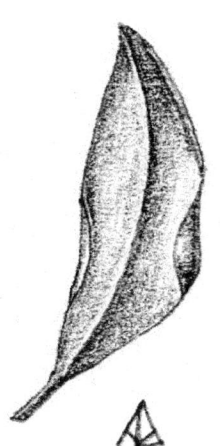

cross time
split asunder in the
infiniverse

first day of winter—
an icy gust rips
through the crack in my heart

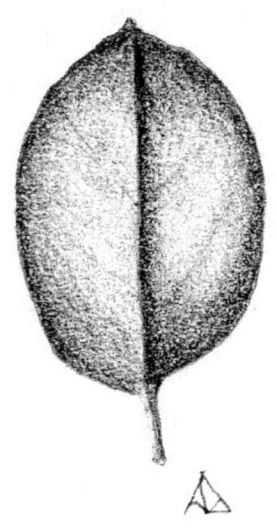

one last strawberry
in the basket
gossip-stained lips

Why, did I believe
You were once part of my soul?
Pieces do not fit.

Pacific kelp bed
Slow motion seaweed forest
Garibaldi home

Poem for Pj, or one
of fifty owed for my love
sappy confessions

of admiration, allure
endless luminosities

candle burns down
to a glowing pool of wax
memories lost in the air

a henro hike
wears down my body
yet lifts my soul

last night on earth
still dreaming
of the red planet

silent soaring birds
over cliffs on sea breeze lanes
pelicans roam free

You are the first bite
of a just ripe peach with juice
squishing through my teeth

sleeping out -
I step
up stars

A stone Buddha head
meditates amongst the roots
of ancient banyan.

Red-handed after
I forgot the fork—
blushing beet salad

ripe mango -
sucking the moon
white

locked eyes in produce
met in parking lot
then sex at his house

A powder blue egg
nestled near porchlight
since August, last year.

Central Park

A band plays Tom Waits'
"San Diego Serenade"
While a child dances.

His mother waves a blue fan
Beneath the August sunlight.

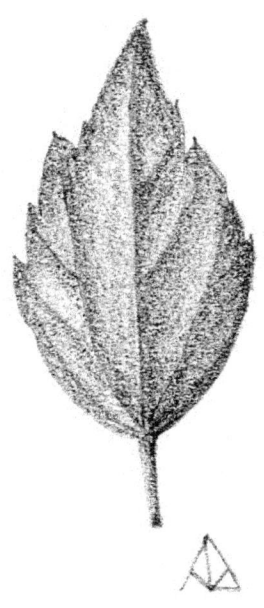

the happiest place on earth

the couple argues
a 90-minute wait time
some kid picks his nose

Ex-Husband

pariah, disgrace
broken promise she left you
alone in the world for years

but she returned a friend
no regrets for my first love.

Tender leaves flutter.
Fresh greens being munched by pest.
Still the plant will grow.

family tree
cut to the ground—
DNA results

Algorithms dance
to spinning light reflected
Cosmic disco ball

Gardenia blooms,
Wax leaf privet gently breathes
Early summer's hope

people whispering
that she shouldn't wear that dress
at the funeral

windblown
the leaves
sing

A smear of blood. We
change the bed linens. This, too,
we put behind us.

my breath comes faster
and I writhe to press closer
my lips part to yours

but we don't kiss—we only
breathe in the space in between

inside candlelight
beneath shadows of empty
pages; torn, yellow, frayed

I was on the couch
in multiple dimensions
talking about plants

Faceless

his warm hands touch strings
and the wooden masterpiece
sings to living flesh

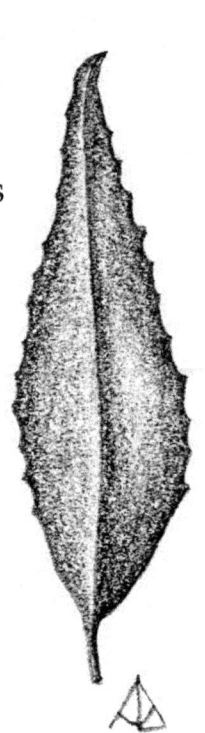

Steel nib on paper,
a working pen surrenders
its life to the hand.

the cool wind on my
face - this skin I will give back
  when I'm through with it

Drought infestation
Swallowed the plum tree. Two stumps
Pucker an orange pot.

a sold out sign
where the lemon trees should be
he plants a lime

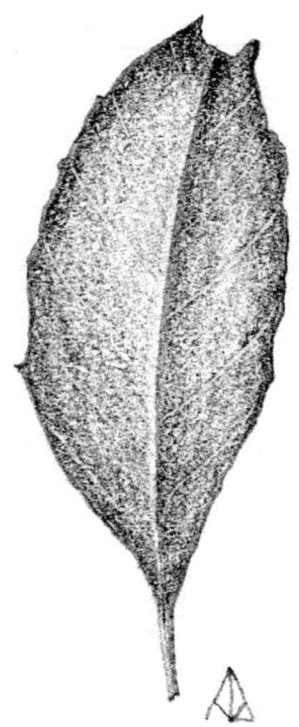

Morning sun flashes
green lizard's throat a red flag:
at dusk, still no mate.

Au Revoir

A French film gave me
the idea to jerk off with
dynamite, le sigh.

Grouse calls,
Canadians tell me,
sound like distant

mooses—proof that love
is the same all over.

Once upon a time
a cat married a princess,
fathered a daughter,

taught her to hunt for small prey.
Mixed children eat their food raw

face the bitter truth
a robot will do your job
better than you can

as this android-written poem
so clearly demonstrates

"Just get over it.
Your problems do not exist
Nor, Anxiety."

The ant meanders—
crossing blue lines on paper,
he enters the poem.

Mirror-Mirror

on the wall, who is
is who is, who is the wall,
a mirror is who

Stars linger coastal
tides pull and sway them across
black sky horizons

Flash of crimson koi
disturbs the pond's surface and
I wake up, gasping.

I make sure my sighs
never cross your wide ocean
because I'm breathing

over a spider web I
am trying not to destroy

Bios

Wondering where all this gray hair has come from. I think I know.
Kareem Tayyar—pages 24, 43, 55, & 89

D'ellen writes poetry because it's cheaper and more effective than going to therapy.
pages 58, 71, 73, & 93

Dean Okamura is exploring haiku and other poetry. He lives in Torrance, California.
pages 40, 78, 79, & 81

---

bardonaut
exploring the multiverse
through poetry
outer and inner worlds
united in fantasy
Charles Harmon—pages 6, 50, 80, & 111

Alexandra Umlas is the author of At the Table of the Unknown.
pages 11, 57, 90, & 106

Zack Nelson-Lopiccolo drinks beer from snifters, flings flies into sub space corridors and cuddles cats.
pages 12, 67, 77, & 100

Burt Shultz, a rogue and world traveler in a time before our time.
pages 3, 10, 56, & 72

Deborah P Kolodji writes haiku while she is sleeping and when she's awake.
pages 19, 48, 49, 62, & 74

Early mornings
sprinklers hiss
cats coffee poetry
Penelope Moffet—pages 13, 28, 36, & 85

Nadia Davi is a control freak whose favorite words are swagger and acetylcholine.
page 108

Tad Wojnicki admins his "Haiku On The Riad" & "Erotic Haiku" groups on Facebook.
pages 54, 63, 83, & 86

I'm Danny. It's my first time writing haiku for publication. Please be gentle!
Daniel Ta—pages 34, 39, 52, & 69

Kitty Anarchy is an anarchafeminist, chicana womyn poet and short story writer.
pages 1, 59, 87, & 96

Francesca Borella, a writer of poetry and memoir to make sense of life.
pages 31, 45, 53, & 92

Suddenly, All Hell Broke Loose!!! by **Brian Harman** will be released this fall.
pages 16, 64, 101, & 114

Lloyd David Aquino writes, teaches, and lives with his dogs Charlie and Brady.
pages 21, 35, & 88

---

an emerging voice—
Aruni Wijesinghe
sometimes writes haiku
pages 61, 84, 98, & 116

A. C. Park works in a library and studies Creative Writing at UCR.
pages 27, 30, 102, & 103

Marcyn Del Clements converted her swimming pool into a swimming pond, with koi.
pages 5, 14, 41, & 60

John Brantingham, the first Poet Laureate of Sequoia and Kings Canyon National Park.
pages 29, 38, & 109

LeAnne Hunt publishes a blog on writing prompts that she doesn't use. Doh!
pages 15, 33, 94, & 110

Betsy Mars is finally fulfilling childhood dreams of writing, doctoring animals, and travelling.
pages 44, & 51

Francesca Terzano loves cats and to write.
pages 26, 65, 75, & 112

Kevin Ridgeway's poems tend to get around the world more than he does.
pages 37, 46, 47, & 91

Steven Hendrix reads, writes and lives in San Francisco with wife and son.
pages 17, 18, 68, & 104

MFA 2012 CSULB: lecturer UH, Kaua'i; married Erik Horsely 2017; dances; gardens; paints.
Nicole Street—pages 2, 42, 107, & 113

Bill Mohr teaches 20th century American Literature at California State University, Long Beach.
pages 9, 25, 66, & 105

K. Andrew Turner writes queer and speculative fiction, poetry, and nonfiction.
pages 22, 23, 32, & 115

Susan is always writing the same poem without ever using the same words.
Susan Vannatta—pages 4, 8, 20, & 82

Lee Anne McIlroy is a professor, linguist, writer, mother, animal lover and friend.
pages 7, 70, 76, & 95

Terry Ann Wright reads, writes, teaches, eats, drinks, and loves: passionately and wildly.
pages 99, & 117

Acknowledgements

face the bitter truth first published online in the Atlas Poetica Science Fiction Tanka feature, April 2018

The ant meanders first Published 2012 in Bank Heavy Press

www.ingramcontent.com/pod-product-compliance
Lightning Source LLC
Chambersburg PA
CBHW060159050426
42446CB00013B/2905